The Dictionary of Dads

With love to Juliet, Joss, Woody and Rufus who inspired these poems. And for my own Abracadabra Dad.

Text copyright © Justin Coe 2017 except
Daddy Disaster © Justin Coe 2012
Spoon-Feeding Dad © Justin Coe 2009

Illustrations copyright © Steve Wells 2017

First published in Great Britain and in the USA in 2017 by
Otter-Barry Books, Little Orchard, Burley Gate, Herefordshire, HR1 3QS

www.otterbarrybooks.com

A catalogue record for this book is available from the British Library.

ISBN 978-1-91095-916-9

Illustrated with line drawings

Set in Garamond Premier Pro

Printed in Great Britain

9 8 7 6 5 4 3 2 1

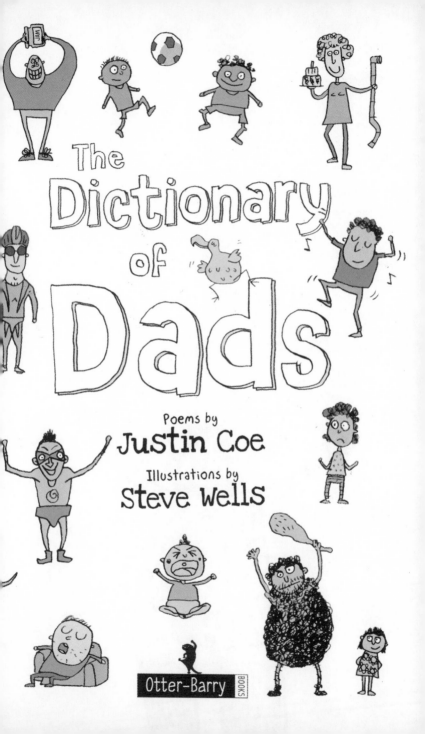

The Dictionary of Dads

Poems by
Justin Coe

Illustrations by
Steve Wells

Otter-Barry BOOKS

Contents

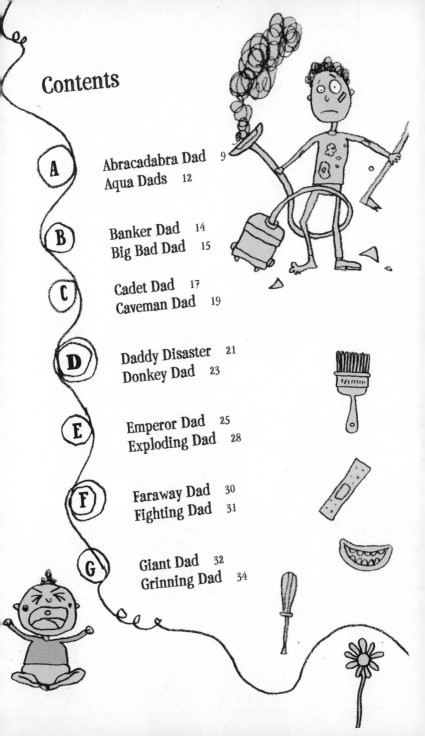

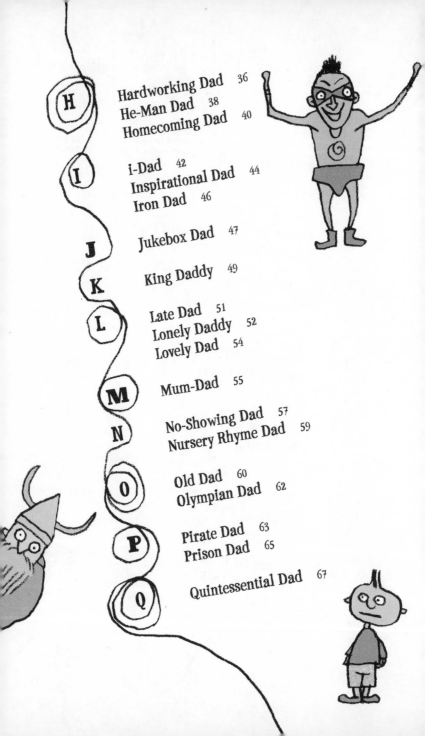

Abracadabra Dad

He's my Abracadabra dad
He wows me with his wizardry
Slips secrets up his sleeve
To magic away misery

He's a genius of japes and jests
He's full of giggly-jokery
He takes the words out of my mouth
And turns them into poetry

Any random thing you say or sing
Or any sight you're seeing
Even far-fetched fantasy
He can bring it into being

He hides the skies in his eyes
The moon in his moustache
The stars shine on the ceiling
With one flick of his brush

He dips a hand into his hat
And raises up a rabbit
He could make a dodo dance
And an omelette while he's at it

He tips the world upside-down
Stands on his head to view it
Fires flowers from his trouser legs
Says that's the way to do it

And when I'm winded, wounded
Bruised or broken-hearted
He turns my tears to Fizzy-Aid
And gets the party started

He's a whizz of many wonders
Though he and I agree
Of all his marvels conjured
The most marvellous is...

ME!

Aqua Dads

Daddies of the pools,
daddies of the oceans,
plucky daddy penguins,
puckish daddy dolphins.

Treading the deeps
with the grace of an octopus
or wading the shallows
like hippopotamus.

Bubble-blowers, dinghy-towers,
splash-fanatics, squirters,
nose-dippers, wave-skippers,
weekend fun surfers.

Skinny daddy pipefish,
wobbly daddy whales,
barking like sea lions
or shy in their shells.

As awkward on land
as the duck-billed platypus
but joyous and buoyant
in the big bath of happiness.

Armband-puffers, stroke-instructors,
shark-impersonators,
splish-sploshers, belly-floppers,
playful alligators.

In case of endangerment
we must take good care of them.
Let's build them a tank
at the local aquarium.

Banker Dad

Welcome to the Bank of Dad
The bank you don't have to get out of bed for
The bank that likes to say "Help yourself"
The bank that can always be persuaded
The bank that believes in your dreams
The bank that has been investing in you since
   before you were born.

All transactions are legitimate with a
   birth certificate
All you need to do is say the magic word
Pay no fees
Pay no charges
Pay nothing back to
The bank you can talk to
The bank you can trust...

The Bank of Dad is the bank to turn to
Until the Bank of Dad goes bust.

Big Bad Dad

(After Big Bad John by Jimmy Dean and Roy Acuff)

Us kids all knew our daddy was strict
He was hard as bones, he was tough as brick
But none of us knew what made him tick
And we was all sure not to give any lip to Dad
Big Dad, big Dad, big bad Dad

He kept us fed and he kept us dry
But I was scared of him, he made me shy
He was built like a building up to the sky
It was hard for us to see eye to eye with Dad
Big Dad, big Dad, big bad Dad

When we were born he was filled with pride
But he kept his distance, stayed outside
And even on the night his mamma died
I heard him sniff but he never cried, did Dad
Big Dad, big Dad, big bad Dad

Then one day he turned the radio on
And on came a Country and Western song
He slapped his thighs and he whooped along
When he began to weep we thought something's
   wrong with Dad
Big Dad, big Dad, big bad Dad

Now he's bought himself a steel guitar
And a pick-up truck (he's ditched his car)
He line-dances down at the Cowboy Bar
And when he walks through the door he goes
  YEEHAA, does Dad
Big Dad, big Dad, big bad Dad

He's a big oak tree in touch with his roots
He's got a Stetson hat, stirrups on his boots
His gun is loaded but he never shoots
And if we laugh, he doesn't give two hoots,
  'cos he's Dad
Big Dad, big Dad, big bad Dad

Cadet Dad

Sergeant-Major – ready for inspection.
Daddies to be – stand to attention.

Now, let's have a look – what have we got?
Tut tut tut, what an 'orrible lot.

Belly in, boy – look at that beer gut.
As for you, lad, go 'n' get your 'air cut.

Left, Right, Quick March, don't be a quitter.
You'll be a dad soon, better get fitter.

Pick up the paintbrush, sell your guitar.
Knees bend, arms stretch, rah rah rah.

Put your pushchair in
Pull your pushchair out
In out, in out, shake it all about
Rock the little baby when you put it down
It's gonna scream and shout... oi!

Wakey, wakey! What's the time?
Three in the morning... rise and shine.

Best be ready when it comes to get you.
Don't let the sick or the snot upset you.

Stink bomb's gone off! It's a beauty!
Come on, soldier, do your duty.

Learn the drill, obey your orders.
The nursery now is your headquarters.

So face the facts, the baby's coming.
Stand to attention, there's no use running.

Caveman Dad

He comes out of his cave
in a bearskin rug,
shouting, "Behave!"
and waving his club.

My dad the caveman
A gruff and grave man
The rant and rave man
My caveman dad

He eats what he kills
and he draws what he thinks.
He's got hundreds of skills
but he's hairy and stinks.

My dad the caveman
Don't-wash-and-bathe man
Won't-have-a-shave man
My caveman dad

His eyes scream Beware,
he scares off the teachers.
But we know that he cares
'cos he never eats us.

My dad the caveman
He's nobody's slave man
An honest and a brave man
My caveman dad

Daddy Disaster

He lives in a house that's all lopsided,
where the chores aren't done and the drawers
    aren't tidied.
His car is wrecked and his driving's reckless,
his favourite outfit is his breakfast.
How did he get to become a father?
Boys and girls, it's Daddy Disaster!

The hand he lends is crammed with thumbs,
one job to do's too much at once.
Who broke the bath? Do you have to ask?
Can he fix it? No, he can't.
If you want to make a mess, then meet the master.
Welcome to the world of Daddy Disaster!

Who cut himself on a pencil sharpener?
Coloured his face in fluorescent marker?
Set his hair on fire with a harmless sparkler?
Sat his bottom down on a wet banana?
Yes, you must've guessed the answer...
Ladies and gentlemen – DADDY DISASTER!

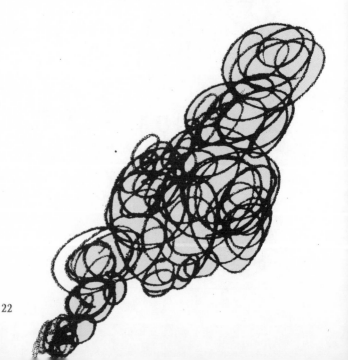

Donkey Dad

Put down your Action Man. Put down your Barbie.
Roll up, roll up for the Daddy Donkey Derby.
Jump on your daddy's back, the race has begun,
Jump on your daddy, quick, the race will be fun.

They're under starter's orders – and they're off!
Daddies are complaining that the strain is too much,
But they've got to get to the finish, they can't give up.
They all want to win the Daddy Donkey Derby Cup.

Some say it's a cruel sport and this race must be ended.
Some say it's our heritage and it must be defended.
But it's also great fun and it's ever so thrilling
When you round the last bend and you're so close
    to winning.

All the daddy donkeys look utterly defeated.
None of them won because all of them cheated.
It's been a farcical debacle, a load of old malarkey
But the kids are ALL winners at the Daddy Donkey Derby.

Emperor Dad

Make way for the Emperor Penguin,
King of Dads!

Mum has laid the egg
and now she must rest
far away in the sea.
It is Dad's turn
to stand firm
and do his duty.

All hail the Emperor Penguin,
King of Dads!

Huddling beak against back
on Antarctic ice amongst
his brothers, to survive
the bleak winter wind and
the 64 dark days to come,
he balances the egg
on his feet.
He cannot feed,
he can barely move.
He must stand strong.

All hail the Emperor Penguin,
King of Dads!

If he loses his grip
or the egg is exposed
to the cold,
his chick will die.
But Dad is dedicated,
Dad is focused,
always looking out,
always listening out
for the call of his mate
as the shell cracks open...

All hail the Emperor Penguin,
King of Dads!

A fledgling penguin is born,
this time a son,
and Dad must hold the chick close
under the cloak of his wing
to keep him from harm.
He feeds him
everything he has,
from the back of his throat,

and they wait...
until at last
Mum comes, calling,
greeting her chick
with a bellyful of fish.

Her newborn Emperor,
kept warm all winter
at the feet
of his father.
It's a super-penguin effort.
And he rarely fails.

All hail the Emperor Penguin,
King of Dads!

Exploding Dad

"If you don't come here by the count of THREE,
you'll see an altogether nastier side of me,"
snapped Dad,
cross and at a loss for words to measure
the very depths of his displeasure.

But Veronica played dumb,
chewed her gum
and continued to be bad.

"Right," growled Dad, "don't make me mad."
He began to count... "ONE!"

But still she did not come.

Dad's anger only grew
until there was nothing he could do
but shout out, "TWO!"
At which Veronica laughed.

"TWO AND A HALF!"
roared Dad.

But, sad to say,
Veronica stuck out her tongue and walked away.

And although Dad knew he was being daft
he thought to give her one last chance.
"TWO AND THREE QUARTERS!"

But still she would not listen to his orders.

Finally, his patience all eroded,
"THREE!" he expounded.
And then he

exploded....

The lesson to learn
and the moral of this verse
is to listen to your dad
if you don't want him to burst.

Faraway Dad

Tonight Dad's staying in another house.
You're at home with Mum but he's someplace else.
He thinks of you with every breath.
It isn't you who he has left.

It's too empty for sleep in this faraway room.
He draws back the curtains, looks up at the moon.
This old moon, he thinks, is the same old moon
That shines down on you and lights your room.

Dad stares at the moon all through the night.
He wishes the moon would shed some light
On how you are. Are you all right?
If only the moon could hug you tight.

He asks the moon to keep you safe,
To pull you through and mend your faith.
Until the dawn defeats the dark
The moon is all he has to ask.

Tomorrow's sun will soon kick-start
A new beat for a broken heart.
He mouths your name on every breath.
It isn't you who he has left.

Fighting Dad

I saw my dad on the telly last night,
fighting for us and his rights.
I thought, *He's a hero –*
but a little bit weird though...
what's with the mask and the tights?

DADDIES AREN'T BADDIES

Giant Dad

Tender as a teddy bear
Stuffed with fluff
He'll hug you hard
With a bellyful of love

Then he curses worse
Than words can spit
He hits you harder
Than hurt can hit

Built like a giant
Rules like a tyrant
He stomps through the house
And the house goes silent

He's tall as the beanstalk
Touching the sky
He's wide as the walls
And the world outside

He's funny and scary
And dark as a clown
And he built this house
And he could knock it down

Built like a giant
Rules like a tyrant
Shouts so loud
That the street goes silent

But the nights will pass
And the day will come
When I grab what's mine
And I run

      run

        RUN.

Grinning Dad

Big Grinning Man points up at the sky and
    yells, *"Plane!"*
Big Grinning Man points out a firework and
    shouts, *"Bang!"*
Big Grinning Man points at a train and says,
    "Choo-choo!"
And he sings, *"The wheels on the bus go round
    and round all day long!"*
until it goes round and round my head
    all day long.

But Big Grinning Man is funny,
pushing me along in the buggy
and talking nonsense.

What's Big Grinning Man doing now?
Upside-down on the climbing frame, waving?
Blowing his nose on a nappy?
With an elephant on his head when it should
    be a hat?
Even I know that.

And sometimes, when Big Grinning Man
points at a spoon and says *"Plane!"*
I think, 'Where's your brain, Big Grinning Man?
When's the last time you slept?
Hey, don't shout at me, don't forget
you're the Big Grinning Man.
And anyway, Big Grinning Man,
how did you get such a big grin?'

I'd like to think it was me who gave him that.
But it's probably just wind.

Hardworking Dad

The dishes are washed
The dishes are stacked
The sandwiches pickled
The sandwiches packed

The bath has been run
The teeth have been brushed
The hair has been washed
The babies all hushed

The housework's all done
The homework completed
Disputes have been muted
The nits have been treated

The dog has been walked
The fish have been fed
The milk has been heated
The stories are read

The carpet's been cleaned up
The shoes are all polished
All of the tasks have been
Ticked off as promised

The toys have been tidied
The kids are in bed
So it's OK now, Dad...

Come out of the shed!

He-Man Dad

If you can't open the jar of jam
I know a man who surely can.
Who can?
He can!
HE-MAN DAD

Who can run faster than
a dog after a burger van?
Who can?
He can!
HE-MAN DAD

Who can out-rock Supergran?
Sink a box of Master Bran?
Who can?
He can!
HE-MAN DAD

Who can make the baddies scram
when they hear the door go slam?
Who can?
He can!
HE-MAN DAD

If he can do it then I can.

A few more press-ups then I am

He-man

Who man?

The man!

You man?

Me man!

I am

HEEEE-MAN DAD

Homecoming Daddy

He's bored of being seen as the baddy
He's hurrying home 'cos he misses us madly
He's growing so tired of missing the moment
Not giving the gifts or seeing them opened.

But he's coming home, he's coming home
Daddy's coming home
He's singing this song all motorway long
Daddy's coming home

Mum's in a stress trying to keep the house clean
Her worries whirl round like the washing machine
Dad's got his foot down, hooting at the traffic
Dad's going to get back to calm all the panic.

And he's coming home, he's coming home
Daddy's coming home
He's singing this song all motorway long
Daddy's coming home

Like Odysseus' return to Ithaca
It's been a journey worthy of literature
A long hard week from Monday to Friday
Now his key's in the door and his car's on the driveway.

And he's coming home, he's coming home
Daddy's coming home
He's been singing this song all motorway long
Daddy's coming home

We run down the hallway and greet him with our kisses
He hugs us to the floor, then drags Mum from the dishes
He's got bridges to build, he's got flames to douse
He's our homecoming dad and he's IN THE HOUSE.

And he's coming home, he's coming home
Daddy's coming home
He's been singing this song all motorway long
Daddy's coming home

i-dad

I'm taking my i-dad back,
it's incompatible with my lifestyle.
All those annoying pop-ups
popping up,
moaning at me to clean my teeth.

I'm taking my i-dad back,
its memory clogged up to its mega-bytes
with my embarrassing history
(all my mishaps
remembered in hi-res snaps).

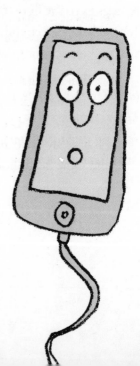

I'm taking my i-dad back,
that i-dad player with its endless
lessons on life, lessons on life
on constant repeat.

I'm taking my i-dad back,
so old fashioned and slow.
I'm sick of the wallpaper
it won't let me change.

Mr Shopkeeper,
please don't shake your head and say *sorry,*
it's the only one you can have,

'cos I'm saving my street-cred
and taking back my i-dad,
saying bye-bye, Dad.
I'll have an i-pod and i-pad
and some headphones instead!

Inspirational Dad

I'm a male marmoset, I don't monkey around.
When it comes to my young I keep them safe and sound.
My bond's been strong since before their birth,
I'm provider, protector, midwife and nurse.

For four long months I was pregnant with pride.
I stayed with my mate, I stood by her side.
I was there at the birth, my teeth cut the cord.
The World's Best Dad? I could win that award.

I carried our twins for weeks on my back,
I kept them clean and safe from tiger attack.
Got food in, did the grooming, showed them my loving.
Then I taught them to be strong with my rubbing and
    my cuffing.

I'm no aloof uncouth orang-utan.
I'm not the *King of Swing* or the big *I Am*.
I'm part of the family and the part I play
is to be there for my babies and never stray.

I'm provider, protector, midwife and nurse.
My bond's been strong since before their birth.
When it comes to my young I keep them safe and sound.
I'm a marmoset male, I don't monkey around.

I'm a male marmoset, I don't monkey around.
As a father to marvel, I'm world renowned.

Iron Dad

The only hugs we had from Dad
Were when West Ham United scored
The only cuddles amongst the bubbles
As the home crowd roared

He was a lion with an iron heart
But a win would make him soften
Those goals were golden moments
I wish they'd scored more often

Jukebox Dad

He dusts down the DJ decks
The hits are heard again
The sounds rebound around and round
Jukebox Daddy's brain.

The gold ones are the old ones
Though jaded and Jurassic
The ages haven't faded them
Every line's a classic.

What time do you call this?
Why can't you tell me the truth?
Do you think I'm made of money?
As long as you're under this roof...

Don't talk back to your mother
Don't talk with your mouth full
Do you think I was born yesterday?
Do you act like this at school?

They don't make 'em like they used to
Hey, were you raised in a barn?
I'll give you something to cry about
It never did me any harm

Why? Because I said so
I'm not going to tell you again
Don't think you're going out like that
I'M NOT GOING TO TELL YOU AGAIN

The gold ones are the old ones
Though jaded and Jurassic
The ages haven't faded them
Every song's a classic.

He dusts down his DJ decks
The hits are heard again
The sounds rebound around and round
Jukebox Daddy's brain.

King Daddy

"I'm the king of the daddies,
the king of all the daddies!"
said my daddy to the daddies.
"I am the Daddy King."

This news amused his mother,
who went and told his brother
and my most disgruntled uncle cried,
"But I'm the king, not him!"

So the daddies put their crowns on
and they slipped their dressing gowns on
and they dashed down to the playground
to settle up the score.

My dad blew a giant raspberry.
It drew a great big gasp from me.
But when Uncle threw a gooseberry,
then I declared a draw.

But going for the killer blow
Dad came back with a pillow throw.
He slipped though, and the pillow split.
There were feathers on the wind.

So, feeling rather flustered,
Dad aimed his gun of custard
straight at my uncle's eyeballs,
but Uncle only grinned.

And so certain he would win it,
he laughed daftly for a minute
till a plastic chicken hit him.
Most amusing, I admit.

While upon the final whistle
Dad fired his water pistol,
drenched Uncle to his underwear.
What a wonder hit!

It was then the contest ended,
and both of them pretended
they were the king of daddies,
they were the Daddy King.

Until the mummies showed up
and told them both to grow up.
Their tea was on the table,
it was time that they went in.

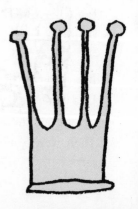

Late Dad

Daddy written in flowers

Across the back window of the black limousine

Don't stare too far into the future

Don't stray too long into the past

You're due home

Lonely Daddy

He is a lonely daddy,
the only daddy at the party,
sitting on the stairs
with the coats,
waiting for the end.

He had hoped to be invited
to join in the games,
but his daughter
has her own friends now
and daddies are no longer wanted.

All the mummies huddle together
in the kitchen,
talking about their holidays
and their husbands.
Daddy has nothing to say to them
and they
have nothing to say to him.

He is a lonely daddy,
the only daddy at the party.
But he is glad no other daddy
has come along
because he is not in the mood
for awkward conversation.

Daddy may be lonely
but he finds some consolation
in watching his daughter have fun,
while quietly making his own sweet way
through the puddings.

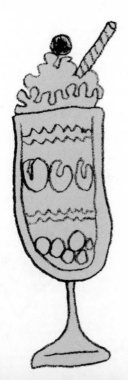

Lovely Dad

(After Walter Dean Myers)

Love my dad
Like a rapper loves to rhyme
Said I love my dad like a rapper loves to rhyme
Mad I never told him
Dad, I'm glad you're mine

He's been here forever
I'm sure he's here to stay
Said he's been here forever and I'm sure he's
   here to stay
And if he should ever leave me
I'm gonna curse that day

Love my dad
Like a singer loves her song
Said I love my dad like a singer loves her song
I'll find a way to say I love him
Before that day has come and gone

Mum-Dad

My mum wears the trousers
And my mum wears the skirts
My mum wears the blouses
And my mum wears the shirts

She takes me to the football
She takes me to the shops
She tells me that she loves me
Even when she tells me off

Mum's all I've ever had
Mum's all I've ever known
And I could not have asked for
A happier home

My mum does the plumbing
My mum cooks the cakes
Mummy keeps the money coming
and she tidies up the place

On Mother's Day it's flowers
On Father's Day it's socks
We cosy up at Christmas
And I'm glad that it's just us

However wild the weather
She's got a way to get it done
And I could not have asked for
A better dad than Mum

No-Showing Dad

My yo-ho-ing dad is a pirate fanatic
My Frodo-ing dad has a hobbiting habit
My snow-throwing dad keeps shouting,
    "Let's have it!"
My show-going dad is over-dramatic

My so-so-ing dad is no saint and no sinner
My hobo-ing dad likes a drink before dinner
My polo-ing dad is much posher and primmer
My slow-going dad has tripped over his zimmer

My oboe-ing dad has a talent worth blowing
My yoyo-ing dad keeps to-ing and fro-ing
My toe-showing dad has socks that need sewing
My slow-mo-ing dad is still out there... mowing

My solo-ing dad is a distant daydreamer
My ho-ho-ing dad is a human hyena
My go-go-ing dad is as lithe as a lemur
My mojo-ing dad is high on Ribena

My dodo-ing dad is dead to me frankly
My no-knowing dad stares at me blankly
My slow-growing dad so longs to be lanky
My nose-blowing dad has got a wet hanky

My cocoa-ing dad loves a cup between naps
My woe-flowing dad tends to turn on the taps
My pogo-ing dad will surely collapse
My no-showing dad will turn up... perhaps.

Nursery Rhyme Dad

Hey diddle doddle
Dad is in trouble
The dog has been sick in the jelly
The baby's distressed, the house is a mess
And the kids have run off with the telly

.

Old Dad

A snow-haired man and his brown-eyed boy
walk through the park.
The man is old,
the boy is three and a half.
It always makes the little boy laugh
when the other people in the park
call his old man 'Grandad'.
The old man nods but puts them straight.
"I'm a grandpa all right but Thomas is my son."
And sometimes the people in the park
don't quite know what to say.
But the beaming lady they bump into today
says, "It's miraculous!"
And the old man looks down at the boy and smiles.

A brown-eyed boy and his snow-haired old man
walk through the park.
It is nearly time to go home.
It is getting dark,
but the old man suggests
this could be the last day of autumn.
So they collect souvenirs
in Thomas's Tank Engine bucket.

They quickly fill the bucket up with
　　autumnal stuff:
pine cones, conkers and acorns.
And on leaving the park,
the boy picks up one last leaf
as a gift for his father.

"Is it mine to keep forever?"
　　the old man asks.
And this time it is his boy's turn to nod and smile.

The old man beams with pride,
holds the leaf gently to his lips
and kisses it,
as if this gift were some kind of
golden ticket.

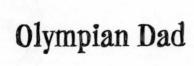

Olympian Dad

My dad is fit, he's the athlete complete.
He cycles up mountains, runs marathons.
My dad's the dad no other dad can beat –
and all agree his talent is Olympian.

A tough-bred thoroughbred born for glory,
his muscles are cogs in an awesome machine.
When writers come to record his story
they'll say he's the greatest the world has seen.

He needs no luck and tries no trickery.
The battles he's been in are battles he's won.
The Goddess Nike carries him to victory
in every race ridden, rowed or run.

But not on my sports day. In the Dad's Race,
he was the fool who fell, with egg on his face!

Pirate Dad

Every Friday evening at five o'clock
my pirate dad docks outside our flat
in his trusty ship, *Ye Olde Rustbucket,*
and blasts the horn.
"Alright, me sailor boy," he says,
and off we sail.

I'm on lookout for coastguards
and enemy gangs.
We have to move fast and
we can't get caught.

Pirate Dad lets me navigate
while he steers the old crate.
"Look for the treasure," he roars.

At the Smuggler's Den
we pick up his girl,
One-Peg Meg.

She's a whizz
on the squeezebox
and we party hard
until morning dawns...

It's been another long weekend on the run,
but when I get homesick for my land-mother
my pirate dad swings the *Rustbucket* around
and the fair winds do the rest.

At the dock he waves me off,
wiping a tear from his glass eye.
"See you next week, sailor boy," he says, and he's gone,
with his songs and his stories
and his unquenchable thirst for glory and rum.

All week long I hold our stormy adventures
close to my heart.
Though we never uncover the X on the map,
never discover the silver and gold,
our pirate days together
are what I treasure most.

Prison Dad

To my Children

This is the hardest letter that I've ever written.
I know I let you down when I was sent to prison.
But, children, listen. I'm not the villain you think I am.
Nor the big hero. Despite my bravado I'm no macho-man.

How can I act hard when these guards have got me sewing?
And, sitting in my cell, I've even started writing poems!
Days go by so slowly. I'm lonely, and the only times
That I find to be close to you are in these rhymes.

'Cos there's no fields inside where we can ride our bikes.
There's no cliff-top here where we might fly our kites.
It's no park-life. There's no slides, no swings...
But who am I kidding? Did we ever even do those things?

I know I let you down. But I am learning to be honest.
I'll make it up to you if you can trust me to keep a promise.
When I was bad it made you sad... if I could change
    all that, I would.
But don't forget, I'll always be your dad.
    And please... be good.

Dad

Quintessential Dad

Teacher, trainer
Temper tamer
All-round clowning
Entertainer

Balloon blower
Party thrower
Grass cutter and
Flower mower

Wound attender
Bruised-mood mender
Play maker and
Great pretender

Room inspector
Lie detector
Home improver
And protector

Wet-nose wiper
Tool provider
Cameraman and
Taxi driver

Trouble queller
Storyteller
Rhyme chimer and
Long-word speller

Big dictator
Decorator
The classic dad –
There's no one greater!

Refugee Dad

Mine were the long hours of labour.
I toiled in the rain and the cold.
But to you I was an alchemist,
I built you a road paved with gold.

Mine was a weary-eyed welcome,
I was the butt of the jokes, and the doors
seemed to shut when I tried to walk through them.
Now yours is the stage and applause.

Mine was the courage of loving
when my faith in my fortune was spent.
When all that I had came to nothing,
yours are the dreams that I dreamt.

Mine was a raft on the ocean
and the nights that couldn't keep out the war.
Mine was the journey, the uncertain journey,
but this land, my children, is yours.

Riddle Dad

The **first** is in teacher but isn't in preacher
It's also in tough but not rough.
The **second**'s in hero, handsome and hairy
But absent in scary or gruff.

The **third** is twice over in cheerful.
It also ends wise and this word.
After a pause the **fourth** begins brave
And the **fifth** is the same as the third.

The **sixth** is in strength and in kindness
And not in a temper too cruel.
The **seventh** is in gallant and gentle and giant,
Thoughtful and tender and tall.

I called him bad words when we fell out
But they swelled up inside me with sadness.
If you link up the letters you'll see that they spell out
The proof and the truth of what Dad is.

Rollercoaster Dad

Oh my Giddy Gosh! Only for you kids
  would I ride this
Shake-and-rattle rollercoaster. I can't hide this

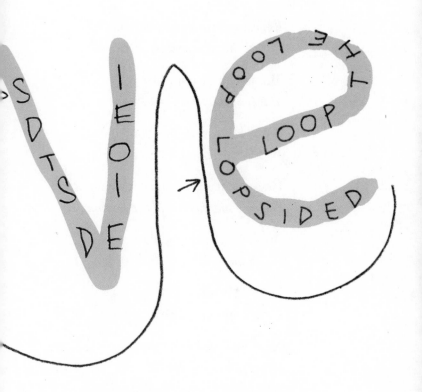

feeling.

That I'm all shook-up is unmistakable.
But the love we share is quite unshakeable.

Sergeant-Major Dad

Repeat this drill and you'll do well
Repeat this drill and you'll do well

This is a house not a hotel
This is a house not a hotel

We all know that life's not fair
We all know that life's not fair

Go mow that lawn and cut your hair
Go mow that lawn and cut your hair

Brush your teeth and flush the loo
Brush your teeth and flush the loo

Do as I say not as I do
Do as I say not as I do

Never slob and never slack
Never slob and never slack
And never answer Daddy back
And never answer Daddy...

Oi! You nauseating nincompoops,
I said DON'T ANSWER ME BACK!
You're all grounded!

Shapely Dad

Mum
Says
Dad's
Tummy
Is like
A Pregnant
Woman's Belly
But my Daddy
Can't have any
Babies only
Ones
Made
Out of Jelly

Soldier Dad

At 6am I should be soundly sleeping,
that's why he never came to say goodbye.
The front door shuts upon my father leaving.
We've played this scene before. I do not cry.

It's just the job he does. He'll soon be back.
It makes us proud to think of where he's gone,
protecting us should enemies attack.
We must sit tight at home and soldier on.

It's in our minds but yet we dare not mention
our worst fears for him lest they come true.
When the phone rings we all stand to attention.
Dad speaks, we sigh relief, then breathe anew.

He's my hero. My father, right or wrong.
Defeat or victory, please come safe home.

Spoon-Feeding Dad

It's the wand of a wizard trying to trick you
It's the tongue of a lizard looking to lick you
It's a squirming worm, it's a wriggling tadpole
It's a spy-ship in space spinning into a black hole
It's a sea monster lurking under the ocean
Preparing to pounce with the spit of its potion
It's a snake sneaking up ready to bite you
It's a circling plane stacked up in a flight queue
It's a train in a tunnel (all together now) *choo-choo*
A rollercoaster ride, hold tight and go *wahooo*
It's a boat by the coast on the edge of disaster
And with the art of a dart but moving much faster
Brum brum! It's a racing car roaring through traffic
Like a moonlit broomstick it's motored by magic
It's a jelly-on-a-spoon race and there's only one winner
Oh, for crying out loud... just eat up your dinner!

Sportsman Dad

Dad's favourite sport
On the couch with the baby
Synchronised snoring

Step-Dad

Not in the shape of our faces
Not in the shade of our skin
Not in the marks or the traces
We make when we groan or we grin

Not in the tint of our eyes
Not in the size of our feet
Not in the timbre of voices
Or the tone of our snores as we sleep

But in the time it took
To read a book
To count the sheep
That helped me sleep

Not in the history
Of how it all happened
Or in Maths' mysteries
Or the puzzles of patterns

Not written in blood type
Not hidden in bones
Not measured by height
Or by chromosomes

But in the footballs kicked
Up and down the pitch
And the time we spent
And what it all meant

Storytelling Dad

Once upon a time,
after a warm bath
and clean pyjamas,
I settled into bed.

Wee Willie Winkie
was banging on the door
but was made to wait.
There was still one last pleasure
to be enjoyed before sleep.

Dad blew the dust off the book
and as if by magic
it began to read all by itself.
Dad himself
disappeared before my eyes,
metamorphosed
into a soulful Mole,
a chatty Rat
and a Badger
who spoke
from deep within his throat,
gruff with authority.

But best of all
was when Dad
turned into a Toad,
a horn-hooting,
toot-tooting,
poop-pooping Toad,
Motor-Car Maniac,
Menace of the Road.

With Toad at the wheel
I couldn't keep still,
couldn't help but ride with him.
I was there,
feeling the fervour beside him,
the whoosh of the wind in my hair,
rushing faster and faster
and faster until –
DISASTER!
We swerved,
hit the curb
and were thrown into the air.

For a moment
I was nowhere.
My eyes closed.
Everything slowed.
Toad and the road gave way
to soft pillows and fresh sheets
as I fell
out of the spell
and into a heap of laughter,

where
I slept deeply

and happily ever after.

Two Daddies

Daddy left and it made me saD
All of us were shocked. Especially NanA
Dad had gone to live with his frienD
Days passed before he calleD
It was hard to understand at first. But now I
Even think it's better to have two dads than onE
So long as we're all happy who cares what anybody sayS

Untidy Dad

When Mum leaves for work
Dad shouts,
"Right, boys and girls,
turn the TV up
and let's get the toys out!"

The balls from the ball pit,
which we kick down the hall.
Then the train set.
And when we get bored of that,
the Scalextrics,
the Lego bricks
and the giant jigsaw with all the titchy jigsaw bits.

Then, after a game of penalties,
Dad decides it's time for elevenses
(though it's only half past ten).

We head straight for the chocolate biscuits
and paint the walls with our handprints.

As usual lunch is a munch on a sandwich
and Dad chasing us about the flat

while we crunch crisps into the carpet.

After the early afternoon's CBeebies snooze
there's no time to lose.
It's paints and crayons and crafts and cars.
Then a quick round of cowboys.
Dad fires a shot from a catapult
and breaks a vase.

Which is when Mum calls.
Work's nearly finished.
She'll be home in ten minutes.

The colour of fun
drains from Dad's face.

Quick!

Pack away the train set, the Scalextrics, the jigsaw bits,
the craft packs, the paints,
the crayons, the catapults, the cars.
Don't forget the balls.
Wipe down the walls.
Scrub the chocolate from our cheeks.
Pick up the crisps from the carpet.
Turn down the TV.
Glue the vase!

When Mum bursts through the door
we are sitting
bolt upright on the sofa, smiling,
posing a photograph
of calm perfection.

Everything looks tidy.
Even the vase
Is holding together.

"Inspection!" laughs Mum.

"No, Mum!" we cry.
"Don't open the cupboard under the stairs!"

Too late.
Mum quickly comes to grief,
buried beneath
the unforgiving avalanche
of all the debris of the day.

"Are you OK?" we ask.
But Mum's moans are drowned out
by the manic sounds of a battery-operated
caterpillar
singing *The Wheels on the Bus*.

Uppity Dad

My dad can be good company
It's rare he has the hump with me

But he can sometimes be quite uppity
If he don't get his cuppa tea

Viking Dad

My dad's dad's dad's dad's dad's dad's dad's
dad's dad's dad's dad's dad's dad's dad's
dad's dad's dad's dad's dad's dad's dad's
dad's dad's dad's dad's dad was a Viking
and I reckon my dad must be quite a lot like him

Wendy-House Dad

My daddy declares,
"It's so delightful having daughters!"
And he takes great pleasure
In playing with all the toys he's bought us.

Every day we play in our pink Pop-up Wendy House.
Daddy says we're so lucky to have such a nice pink
    Pop-up Wendy House.
When he was a boy there wasn't a single toy he
    would've loved more in the whole wide world
than a pink Pop-up Wendy House.
But he was never allowed.

Daddy says it's different now.
And it's all so jolly when he joins us to prepare
our teddy bear and Barbie dolly picnics.
We get out our (only-for-special-occasions) Polka-Dot
    Porcelain Tea-Set in a Basket
and lay out the pretty tablecloth on the playroom carpet.
We always let Daddy pour the tea
because it makes us giggle when he says,
    "Want another? I'll be mother!"
It's ever so much fun!

Daddy was never allowed a Barbie Doll or a Polka-Dot
Porcelain Tea-Set in a Basket when he was young.

Daddy says times have changed since he was a boy,
and since the three of us were born, it's all been a joy.

And what he loves best
is for us all to dress as fairies and princesses.
We've all got the latest Disney dresses.
Even Dad.
He was never allowed to have a Disney
    dress-up before.
His mother said it was against the law.

My daddy says it's a whole new world,
having girls.
And though I can't help thinking to myself
that My Little Pony
is really His Little Pony,
and I sometimes wish
we could just occasionally
play with cars,
it's still a dream having a daddy like ours.

Where every day is such an amazing
   hair-braiding, hoola-hooping,
   hop-scotching, horse-riding, hell-raising
   girl-raising holiday.
Until
Grandma comes to stay.

Daddy wipes off his Hello Kitty lipstick
real quick then.

And whenever she visits,
Grandma makes him ride his motorbike
and bans him from our picnics.

And should Daddy ever get an urge to
   wear one of his dress-ups
he has to put his football shirt on and do
   a hundred press-ups.

Wise Dad

A wise dad always tries
To give his children good advice
But other dads who have more wisdom
Know their children will not listen

Working Dad

By the time he gets home you'll be in bed
Dreaming of those together times – dream on
By the time you wake up he will have left

All those bedtime stories that he once read
With his goodnight kisses – those days are done
By the time he gets home you'll be in bed

The stars he named for you now fill your head
But whatever star it is you wish upon
By the time you wake up he will have left

The bills must be obeyed and children fed
And when pay's as poor as the day is long
By the time he gets home you'll be in bed

You've been busy too. He'll be impressed
But though you long to tell him what you've won
By the time you wake up he will have left

He's more than the man who brings home the bread
You'd tell him, 'You're my dad and I'm your son.'

But by the time he gets home you'll be in bed
By the time you wake up he will have left...

Xmas Dad

Dad is the presents, the wrapping, the ribbons,
Dad is the tinsel, the lights and the tree.
Dad is the table, the turkey, the trimmings.
He's the Father of Christmas to me.

This Christmas as usual he's brewed up the beer.
He's hung up the holly and decked out the hall.
If Dad wasn't here, there'd not be the cheer,
It wouldn't be Christmas at all.

For Dad is the crackers, the talk and the toys.
Dad is the dinner, the drink and the tea.
Dad is the nuts, the farts and the noise.
He's the Father of Christmas to me.

He hasn't the reindeer, the beard or the suit.
He hasn't the sack or the sleigh.
But he sprinkles the dust that's so special to us
And makes Christmas a magical day.

Yelling Dad

If you hear the yell
you can tell you've done wrong.

A yell that rattles the bones of the houses
and sends shivers down the skeleton streets,
pushing the grass aside,
brushing past the leaves,
scurrying through back alleys
like a wild dog snarling.

The yell can sniff you out,
knows where you are hiding.

It rises over the rooftops,
flies on the wind
with *poltergeist* power,
wrestles its way through the trees
into the park,

where you are found
in the penalty box
with your hands on the ball.

The yell wants a word with you, girl.
It's got bad news for you, boy.

You will hear it.

Yeti Dad

Half human and half Grizzly Bear
A bulk of a hulk skulking in hair
A Neanderthal brain and werewolf stare
My dad's a Yeti!

On fangs of teeth his words are mangled
He barks like a dog that's being strangled
His unwashed locks are toughly tangled
Lengths of spaghetti.

He's a horror movie of his own making
When he corners you there's no escaping
His deathly breath and his skin all flaking
Like scab confetti.

He howls through streets at the creep of night
Bloody-nosed from blows in moonlit fights
My friends all ask me if he bites
It does upset me.

Like father, like child! It can't be right
I check my skin for signs every single night
Please, no, don't let me turn out like
My dad the Yeti!

Zen Dad

"What is the best sort of father?"
I asked my Zen Dad Master.

For no one is wiser
than this great adviser.

At first he did not answer,
but rather
stroked his beard and let out a soft burst
   of laughter.

"Who is the best?"
I insisted.

"Is it the proud but distant?
Is it the gentle but indulgent?
The thoughtful and resourceful?
The lenient or the forceful?

Is it the one who stays at home?
Is it the one who goes to work?
Is it the strong and silent one?
Or more like the type
that is playful yet prone to over-excitement?

Please answer, Zen Dad," I pleaded.
But Zen Dad continued stroking his beard.

Nothing was said...

until finally he let out a long
Ommmmmmmmmmmmmmmmmmm

Then it was time for bed.

Zzzz Dad

(Can be sung to the tune of Hush, Little Baby, Don't Say a Word)

Hush, darling Daddy, now don't you fret.
We'll fall asleep soon – but just not yet.

And if your lullabies won't work,
You could always read us a bedtime book.

And if that book doesn't make us snug,
Why don't you find us a teddy to hug?

And if that hug only makes us hot,
You could always pour us a glass of squash.

And if that squash makes us want to wee,
You might as well let us watch TV.

Hush, darling Daddy, let's kiss good night,
We'll put you to bed and we'll turn off the light.

You're much more sleepy than your boys and girls.
But you're still the sweetest Daddy in the whole wide world.

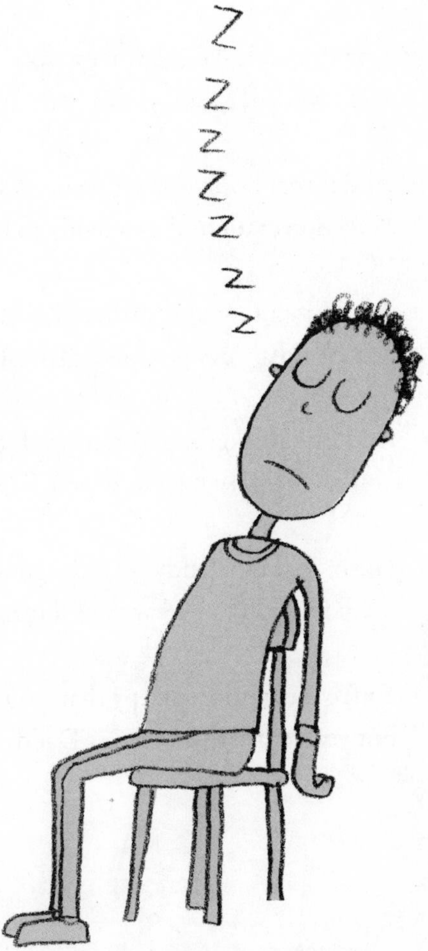
ZZZZZZZ

Acknowledgements

The Dictionary of Dads began life as
'Danny's Dictionary of Dads', a
spoken-word theatre narrative.

Many thanks to Dee Ashworth, former
Artistic Director of the Gulbenkian
Theatre, Canterbury, the Lit-up Live
Literature Consortium and Arts Council
England for supporting this venture.

Special thanks to fellow poet Roger Stevens
for his patient mentoring and skilled advice
on the transformation of the narrative to
this collection of poems.

Daddy Disaster was first published in
Born to Giggle, Save the Children, 2012,
edited by Ian Billings and Hunt Emerson.

Spoon-Feeding Dad was first published
in 2009 on the Wondermentalist website,
edited by Matt Harvey.

About Justin Coe

Justin Coe is a performance poet on a mission to reconnect people with poetry and poetry with people. A regular and popular performer in schools, theatres and community settings, he has entertained everywhere from Sheppey to Shanghai and from the Savoy Hotel to street corners, steam trains and a sitting-room made entirely out of newspaper.

In the last decade, since relocating to Southend and becoming a father, he has also written and performed seven spoken-word theatre shows for young people. His most recent show Big Wow Small Wonder (about the joys of being the smallest boy in school) is produced by Half Moon Theatre in east London and continues to tour to venues nationally.

He first dreamt of writing a book when he was five years old. It's taken him nearly 40 years, but he's done it!

About Steve Wells

 Steve Wells is a Bath-based designer and illustrator who works mainly in publishing. He works for many people, including Chicken House, Scholastic, Mills and Boon and Harper Collins. He has designed over 200 book covers and his spontaneous and scratchy illustrations have appeared in more than a dozen books. His illustrations have been published around the world. He lives in Bath with his wife and three children, one cat and a lizard.

You can see more of his work on Instagram: @stevewellsdesign and his website: stevewellsdesign.com

More great poetry from
Otter-Barry Books

Adder, Bluebell, Lobster
978-1-910959-55-8

Dinosaurs and Dinner-Ladies
978-1-910959-56-5

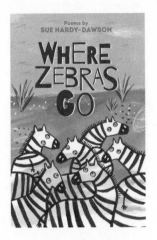

Where Zebras Go
978-1-910959-31-2

How to be a Tiger
978-1-910959-20-6

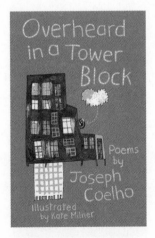

Overheard in a Tower Block
978-1-910959-58-9
(Available July 17)